Illuminated

poems by

Sandra Thaxter

Finishing Line Press
Georgetown, Kentucky

Illuminated

ACKNOWLEDGMENTS

I am grateful to the Newburyport poetry community, the *Powow River Poets,*
the *Ibbetson Street Journal,* who published two poems from this collection,
and its insightful editor Harris Gardner, and to the teachers Rhina Espaillat
and Alfred Nicol with their students and followers.

I also want to thank my family, for their support, and their reading, and
contribution to the visual and selections for this chapbook.

Publisher: Leah Maines
Editor: Christen Kincaid
Cover Art: Sandra Thaxter
Author Photo: Willy Somma
Cover Design: Elizabeth Maines McCleavy
Page 1: Andrew Wyeth, "Spindrift," 1950
© 2020 Andrew Wyeth / Artists Rights Society (ARS), New York

Order online: www.finishinglinepress.com
also available on amazon.com

Author inquiries and mail orders:
Finishing Line Press
P. O. Box 1626
Georgetown, Kentucky 40324
U. S. A.

Table of Contents

*This book is dedicated to the courage of women writers
over the centuries, beginning with Egyptian Queen Hatshepsut
into the present generation, who are still bringing to us
courageous messages of truth, beauty and grace
in the midst of the difficulties and wonder of our time.
I want to recognize the women of FEMRITE in Kampala Uganda
among these authors.*

*I also dedicate this to the humble clover flower growing among
granite at the end of a pier. Its discovery led me to notice how beauty
and grace finds a way to thrive in the harshest of places.*

Dory

Beached at the edge of the tide is a dory,
sculpted of smooth wood. Narrow rails curve
along each side. It's a live thing perched there,
its bow lifted. This dory—like bones left
on a burnished landscape,
where man just happened to arrive
from some other place.

This place, a ruffled crust. Still here is a survivor
from when planets dropped meteors like silent rain.
Left behind, blanched shells. No fish bones for hawks
far away on another plateau, their shadows mere specks.
No other living thing. Here are pale marks of the past,
shapes of a passage. A dory
worn as from years at sea,
rests alone in a tinted world—
in silence beached.

Spindrift by Andrew Wyeth

1

Child of Your Dreams

Spun out
from your night sky
from your dreams
in distant wars and seas.

Here I am, dropped
cold, shivering
on the wet sand,
picking up pieces I find
scattered and strange
at the edge of the strand.

I gather some,
turn over each one
in my wet hand
bits of glass and wood,
worn dark and smooth,
bright pebbles and a scrap of paper.

Did you leave me here
without showing me
where the beach pea grows,
where to pick the sorrel,
or how to sing out the snails?

I lay the pieces out
one by one,
consider their place—
as words on a page
each fitting in its space
to assemble the story,
to make them speak.

Here I stay, here I dwell,
looking to each one to tell
of their coming here,
to make this their place—
to spell me out—
the child of your dreams.

Singing the Snails by Sandra Thaxter

Winter Morning

From the east through my window,
the air is still as ice—the glass crisp
with crystal webs that sparkle. Light
streams through a shield of frost.
It strikes a spray of purple buds
in the window and lights them up.
Shadows of their long stalks spread out
against the wall where a photo hangs.

There in the photo my children and I
hover together against wind on a beach.
My lips press my crying infant's cheek
in hope that his tears will subside.

Warmth rises, like a summer's heat
on this sand colored wall where shadows meet.
The buds' purple flowers bloom as a mother's care
hovers around the child in her windblown lair.

Love Tangles

The letters you had kept for forty years,
deep in troubled darkness hidden away.
You found them in boxes nestled together.
And did you say there were hundreds?
How could we have written them all?
Your carefully rounded cursive rolling
across so many yellow legal sheets.
Were there signs of love in this long discourse?
I tremble at the me then, what I know now,
the me of those long retorts scrawled out.
So many words, collisions of beliefs and fears?
The constancy of twisted, tangled thoughts,
lie soft with age, like woven roots covered with moss,
beneath thickening sod.

The Knitting

Two balls of yarn and a half knitted sock
still nestled in mother's basket,
carried like a child's first gift
from house to house into the spring,
hoping for a day to knit again.

I must take into my hands
the soft pink wool, its strands
years ago sun-soaked in the juice
of wild strawberries that drew us
to Cape Breton's windblown coast.

I want to feel the soft curl of yarn
as it turns into a stitch of purl
in a row abandoned long ago,
those days we thought would always be.
How could we know how lives can go astray?

I must take the knitting into my hands,
now speckled with the marks of age,
The yarn still on the needles,
still held through many tangled years,
and rivers of loss and unshed tears.

Side by side each row of pink and white,
Still steady, the stitches tight.
The patient pink holds its place
beside the wool's own natural hue.
It soothes as deep as night's darkest blue.

I sigh as my fingers ply a thread
and lift the needles, how fitting
a reminder, not to leave the knitting.

Cape Breton by Sandra Thaxter

House on the Hudson

I found a poem you wrote
from the tiny house on the Hudson,
your final year of college.
"A long dry season," it said.

I remember my visit there
to that house near the river,
and our walk in the sinking sun
through a field sweet with grass.
We shuffled beneath the maples,
turning over new-fallen leaves,
trying out some words to say—
to break the ruffle of unease.

That evening we cooked
some rice and mango curry.
We chatted and stirred the stew.
The room was cozy and bright
and I brought out my gift,
a small square computer.
I turned on its little soft light,
a place to write, to make
a life of small things.

When I got up and turned around
to refill my plate, I tripped
against a mirror leaning there.
It broke. "Ten years of bad luck,"
you said without a tear.
We piled up the pieces,
and ate our dinner.

In the morning sun broke through
the trees as we carried the shards,
dropped them into the eddies
one by one, and watched them slowly sink.
I only know the moments,
the angle of light, a look in your eyes,
that pulls a shard
from deep down.

Song of the Soul

It is just a whisper
that rides on the evening air.
It brushes our cheeks,
a flush of warmth,
just a breath—
like a long-lost melody—
from songs we once knew.
Words rise in our throats,
but we are unable to form a note,
silenced by a wave of blush.

I watch my son as the blush
rises, the comfort of hot tears.
Unwilling to name itself,
this rush of love for her—
a lift of the breeze?
Now it is gone, scattered
as milkweed silk
carrying its seeds
on the wind.

Coffee Grounds

Yesterday's coffee grounds cling
to the brown paper,
hold a bitter taste
that still lingers
from yesterday.

What stirred in my bones
in this morning's chill?
Is it some unpaid bill,
the impatience of a friend,
or a promise I didn't keep?

Never assume we have found
what stayed lingering so
in the smell of the leftover grounds.

The brown filter remains
speckled with them.
Still the possibility remains
for another steamy cup.
Bitter, or sweet.

Dust to Dust

In the cracks of brown earth
that traverse the plains,
is Colorado's ancient face.
A strong woman's life,
daughter of the mines,
once braced against the land.

Her face was deeply carved
from leaning towards the plains,
from gazing at the peaks she knew,
gathering her final yearning.
She is gone, her life, dust in small crevices.
Here dust finds its place
in endless wrinkles of rock and sand.

The Rookery

In honor of Sylvia McLaughlin, one of the founders of Save the Bay San Franciso. She lived in the Berkeley Hills and always wore red.

Her terrace is perched on a sunny hillside,
open to a view of the expansive bay
and the distant rising of the Golden Gate.
Here hawthorn trees are thick and thorny,
aflicker with orange, brown and red birds,
trilling in the early morning,

A house finch lives here. She raises her beak
and puffs up and stretches her neck to watch.
Two giant redwoods rise to the sky—
they are the first to know of weather,
to feel the wind, and storms pass by,
to receive the sunrise waking the bay.
This red breasted finch readies for the day.
This is her inheritance, her land's heartbeat.

The sun comes early here. Fog, still cool,
lays its damp below, spreading its breath
over abundant marshes and tide pools.
She turns a fierce gaze at the low baritone
honking of ships and urban rumble.
She sees the tall stacks of billowing black,
so croaks and chirps, and spreads her stories,
of marshes where she was born, the glories
of the marsh flower, the salamander, the frog
the ducks, the hawks, all winged things.
where buzzing and humming sings and rings.

Marsh Grass by Willy Somma

The Inauguration

You welcomed me. You, so tall
and black, standing with me
under the tree, on a summer day;
you, the flower of another garden.
A red blossom you wear catches light,
as you turn your face away,
remembering Obama's first
inauguration day. We talk—

You say it was the first time
you felt you were American.
I remember my deep longing
to know you. The many faces
of the yous caught in my memory.
Now you lean back, and speak.
I receive the sweet shower
of your story, your change of heart
on that inauguration day.

So many women wept that day.
Tears streamed down
many black shining cheeks.
The school bands from the Bronx
and Georgia marched. They blew
their trumpets and banged their drums
for President Barak Obama,
his first Inauguration Day.

Now we are here together.
For so long we lived apart,
you on the other side of the town,
on other buses, in other schools.

I remember watching snowy TV newscasts—
of screaming crowds that spat
on children like you, children with dreams.
I remember the angry men, their bulging bellies
and twisted mouths, shouting at black girls,
shy, neatly dressed, just going to school.
Fire hoses shot water in thundering streams
because you were black, because you had dreams.

Now we can begin to imagine
our life in each other's kitchens,
the warmth of steaming cornbread. Beans
and rice, spices from far places,
my apple crisp, your collard greens?
Our inauguration.

Lamassu* Speaks

For millennia I have stood.
I, Ur of this land and its peoples,
of its great rivers,
of its desert and mountains.

On this ancient earth
I still stand,
my feet sunk deep
into its heart,
beneath the moving skies.
My eyes scan the land
looking toward the rivers,
the rivers that flow long and far,
from the Mediterranean to the Gulf.

The winds brought to me
words spilling like rivers rushing,
words sung from rooftops to hilltops
gathered from the stone temples,
from the tablets and tombs.

Of this earth,
I know the smell
of orchards' once succulent fruit
and the perfume of flowering gardens.

Now they are but dust and dry land
littered with abandoned river beds.
My toes are broken and battered.
The soles of my feet are cracked,
the dust fills my nostrils.
The bones of my people
have been blown from Cairo to Tehran.

This ancient earth now trembles.
My realm for thousands of years
is ripped from its destiny.

*The *lamassu* is a celestial being from ancient Mesopotamian religion bearing a human head, bull's body, sometimes with the horns and the ears of a bull, and wings. It appears frequently in Mesopotamian art.

Nôtre Dame de Paris

April 15, 2019 a fire started in the roof of the cathedral. The spire and much of the roof was destroyed, but the stone structure remained intact.

Nôtre Dame de Paris, mother of our souls,
we gathered beneath your roof.

When our leaders died, you held us.
When our sons failed to return,
you gathered us, sang to us.
When our streets filled with death,
you mourned with us.
When our country was besieged,
you protected us,
In your heart of blue rosettes
beneath carved columns of stone,
you showered us with your light.

You echoed our voices.
You surrounded us with music:
Charpentier, Fauré, Beethoven and Bach,
soaring into the rafters built in your name.
Riches poured into your great naves,
chalices of gold, robes of rich velvet and braid,
kings knelt at your feet, and asked for blessings.

Under your massive roof you sheltered
centuries of prayers that bless this place.
They are held in the worn stone steps,
on marble slabs tred by generations
of rich and poor, shoed and shoeless,
of the bejeweled and of street urchins.
They are held in the stones chiseled by masons,
in the faces of the saints formed in faith
and carved by your sculptors and craftsmen.
who gave their lives and skill with trust in you.

The remains of your great towers are now
the barest of shelters. Maybe it could be enough
to keep our souls, to hold the prayers
laid in this place, Nôtre Dame de Paris.

Geronimo's Bones*

Skull and Bones they called the place
where they had laid Geronimo's bones.

For a while his bones
lay in Oklahoma.
Geronimo, a fierce spirit
who roamed the western plains,
protecting his people's land.

It was a prank, a dare, onetime
paragons of civilized men
dug up his bones to wrest
the power of his myth,
to muscle down the spirit free,
to touch the sun—who knows?

To move bones and tear up stones
will stir souls and shake the earth.

Skull and Bones they call the club.
His bones they buried there
under the floor of their drinking place,
where young Yale men still boast
and toast their manhood, pounding
the floor raising the dust.

Rain in Karen

*Karen is a leafy residential area outside Nairobi named for
Karen Blixen, who wrote 'Out of Africa', one of the early
English accounts of Africa's beauty and people.*

I. The Night

The sky is so big, beyond my sight.
It hangs heavy, dark and deep.
The stars beckon. What do I seek
out here alone in this vast night?

Dogs bark. What do they hear?
Thunder rolls, the rain is near.
It's coming. Who is out there,
as lightning cracks shivering with fear?

Rain rolls down off the eaves,
pounds the walks, and bends the trees.
No mercy here, no place to hide,
from rain that swallows all outside.

Where will all the people go
who hawk their wares along the street?
Will the crowds flow in and out
like schools of fish in rain and heat?

A dog howls in his cage.
Birds screech in escalating rage.
Water rushes down from croton trees
joining roaring torrents in the gullies.

Umbrellas collapse, limbs bow down.
The deluge drowns out all other sound.
My heart is beating, waiting for the end
the trees surround, ghosts not friends.

II. The Dawn

The cicadas' high pitched cries
build to a screech as the dawn arrives.
Their urgent sound scours the sky,
there is no time to let a day go by
without being in full pitch alive,
without taking up the song of the hive.
But this is not the only chorus,
listening to what the day brings for us.
Ripe fruits drop on the earth and lie
in beads of sweat, and dogs stare at the sky

On the Sixtieth anniversary
of the bombing of Hiroshima and Nagasaki

On August 6th, 1945 a nuclear bomb was dropped on Hiroshima.

There was no warning,
there were only victims to witness.

It was a clear blue sky day.
A trim woman
walks in the street
with a large shopping bag.
She looks up
at a plane passing over
low.

In a clean shirt for his work day,
a man gazes out the window
of a tram car.
Another walks briskly,
and grasps the hand
of his small child.
He looks up.

The man up there,
The pilot,
Tibbits was his name
releases the bomb
the special weapon
It explodes
into a great mushroom cloud
on a clear blue sky day.

An invisible wave,
a nuclear bomb
tore through
each city block,
each house,
each small courtyard,
each carefully tended flower bed,
each breakfast table spread in the morning sun.
All burned, melted,
and turned black.
Bodies boiled from the inside.
'Hibashuka' they call them.

The rest of the world
could not hear the cries,
did not know the smell,
did not see the flash, the flesh
of two hundred thousand lives
in minutes gone.

Tibbits,
he felt the wave,
looked—
and flew away
into the clear blue.

Requiem for Women of Light

Two women live as light among stars.
Once their faith and innocence burned bright.
They broke the bonds of men's demands.
They took a step into the armour
and mounted their chariots of fire.
Now in the time of the stars,
their light gathers.

Et lux

There was the maid, Jeanne,
from the town of Arc.
She led the army of France
her banner, a ripple of white
rising from fields of wheat,
toward the dark walls of Orleyans.
Her helmet glittered in the sun.
Her shining spear clove the air.
The army followed her to victory
to regain, the soul of France.
The English lost, but did not submit.
The garlands for Jeanne,
a trial, and a pyre consumed by fire.

Et lux

The other, a teacher, Christa McAuliffe,
in the missile of Man in Space.
Her dream was to reach the moon.
Her vessel, wrought by ambitious men,
rose from the earth and burned.
She was consumed in minutes,
the first woman in space.
Millions of metal shards dispersed
just a trail of white seen streaming in the blue.
The hopes of school children
fell silently to earth.

Et lux perpetua…

Two bright beacons:
Now just particles in the heavens.
shattered reflections of dreams.
Their ashes dropped to the earth
and lie in an evening's still water,
or as the dew in a field of grass,
or laid gently in the hand of a child.

Luceat eis.

*The women are **Joan of Arc** (Jeanne d'Arc), who was burned as
a witch after leading the French army to victory at Orleans. And
Christa McAuliffe, a teacher who won a place on a NASA Shuttle
Challenger to space, by competing with teachers all over the country.
The shuttle exploded 73 seconds after liftoff.
The Latin is from the Mozart Requiem. Et Lux (and light), Et lux
Perpetua (and the eternal light), luceat eis (Grant us the light)*

The Peony by Sandra Thaxter

Sandra Thaxter lives in Newburyport Massachusetts. She was born in Portland, Maine and spends time on an island in Maine.

This is her second published collection. Her poems "Rookery", and "Mirror" have been published by *Ibbetson Street Quarterly Journal*. She studied poetry and writing in New York city at the Poetry Project at St. Marks, and at the 92nd street Y. She also attended the Great Heron Writing Workshop in Antigonish Nova Scotia, with writers from Newfoundland and Cape Breton.

Currently she is studying with Alfred Nicol, and Rhina Espaillat of the Powow Poets. She has attended the Frost Farm Spring poetry weekends in New Hampshire. Her academic background was in languages and comparative literature, as well as software engineering. She worked as a software engineer at Boston area companies including Lotus, IBM, and later at UNICEF.

She says that writing for her is an attempt to tell truths and uncover the struggle and joy that makes us human. She believes that we are formed by the places where we live and learn about ourselves in nature's harsh edges and delicate beauty. She considers poetry as a form of peacemaking, as poetry helps to process the chaos and injustice that is part of our own making.

www.ingramcontent.com/pod-product-compliance
Lightning Source LLC
Chambersburg PA
CBHW050822090426

42737CB00022B/3472